The Wild Man

The Wild Man

A Clear Path for Guiding Boys into Manhood

Fable and Guidebook

By

Zeke Pipher

The Wild Man: A Clear Path for Guiding Boys into Manhood
Fable and Guidebook
Revised Version
© 2024 Zeke Pipher
Printed in the United States of America

Cover and internal artwork by Garrett Rolenc. www.garrettrolenc.com or @garrett.rolenc.art (IG)

Wild Mountain Press. To order *The Wild Man*, visit www.zekepipher.com or your favorite bookseller.

WILD MOUNTAIN

ISBN 978-0-9979627-2-7

About the Author

Zeke is an author, freelance outdoor writer, and pastor. His first book, *Man on the Run: Helping Hyper-Hobbied Men Recognize the Best Things in Life* was published with Howard Books in March of 2012. His second book, *In Pursuit: Devotions for Hunters and Fishermen* was published in June 2014 with Baker Books.

Zeke has been the senior pastor at Heartland Evangelical Free Church in Central City, Nebraska since 2005. He's been married to Jamie since 1997, and together they have three children. Zeke has a Master of Divinity (MDiv) from Talbot School of Theology, and a Doctor of Ministry (DMin) from Gordon-Conwell Theological Seminary.

Zeke's contributed articles and photos to several national outdoor magazines, including *Field & Stream, Deer & Deer Hunting, Petersen's Bowhunting, Bow & Arrow Hunting,* and *Whitetail News.* Zeke is represented by Pape Commons. For more information visit www.zekepipher.com.

"This message could change the world!"

...

"I say that because after spending my life serving the world's most vulnerable populations, I've observed that most pain and suffering can be laid at the feet of men. If they would just step up to be faithful husbands, loving fathers, and dedicated providers, most of this world's hurts could be eradicated. Our ever-shifting cultural definitions of masculinity muddle what it means to be and act like a man, to the point where men can feel they are losing the liberty, and even the instinct, to be themselves—the masculine human beings God created them to be.

In *The Wild Man*, Zeke offers that being a 'real man' is an inside-out issue—it's not based on appearances, or even performance; it can't always be seen or measured. It involves what's going on inside a man's heart, evidenced by his striving to reflect the character and example of Christ. A man never stands so tall as when he stoops to serve others."

➤ **Dr. Wess Stafford**
President Emeritus, Compassion International

"The rapidly changing cultural landscape in America is making the role of parenting ever more challenging. Having meaningful conversations with children on essential issues is one of the challenges for any parent. Zeke Pipher has given fathers a significant gift in *The Wild Man* which provides tools to help initiate and guide these essential conversations with a Biblical foundation. As a father of three grown sons and the grandfather of three young grandsons, I'm thankful to Zeke for his heart to see a generation of young men of God raised up across America."

➤ **Kevin Kompelien**
President, Evangelical Free Church of America

"*The Wild Man* is a wonderfully creative story that helps boys and men consider masculinity deeply. The guidebook provides a clear vision for how they can express their God-given manhood well. Many today think that the only kind of masculinity is toxic masculinity. Zeke has written a study that will go a long way to correct this misconception and establish a biblical foundation to bring clarity to our modern-day confusion.

I'm deeply grateful that Zeke has given us a clear and helpful picture of character traits that all boys should aspire to possess."

►► Dr. Erik Thoennes
Professor and Chair of Theology, Talbot/Biola
Pastor, Grace Evangelical Free Church, La Mirada, CA

"As a father and pastor, I know the struggle to have conversations with our sons about the things that matter most–conversations about identity, purpose, and the acceptable, seemingly innocent dangers lurking in their paths. *The Wild Man* offers men and their sons the pathway of a compelling story and strategic guidebook to fuel these important conversations.

Don't do this alone! The journey is more potent in a community of fathers, grandfathers, mentors, and young men who are using *The Wild Man* as a guide."

►► Larry Austin
Director of Church Health, EFCA Central District

"Every boy's heart longs for a story, an epic adventure. For many young men today, that desire is dimmed by the glow of electronic devices and a hurried lifestyle that neglects this core need. But there are a few men out there, men on a rescue mission to liberate the hearts of the boys, fathers and sons, who long for this together. Zeke Pipher is one of those men and *The Wild Man* fable and guidebook is fantastic! Enjoy the adventure."

▬▬▬▬▶ TJ Greaney
Founder and Owner, Kids Outdoor Zone

"It's easy to bemoan the lack of godly men in this world. I could quickly dash off a paragraph about the pitfalls and failings of 'failure-to-launch' males, no problem. But it's much more difficult to see the problem and then do something constructive about it.

Zeke has 'manned-up' and done the harder thing, creating something valuable that can be used by others to raise up godly men. I love that he wrote the simple, creative story for his son Aidan in the first place as an exercise in faithful fathering. As the father of three growing boys, I am encouraged by Zeke's example to do my own part."

▬▬▬▬▶ Matt Mitchell
Author of *Resisting Gossip*
EFCA Pastor and Book Reviewer

For Aidan, my favorite Wild Man

Contents

"Only men can initiate men, as only women can initiate women. Women can change the embryo to a boy, but only men can change the boy into a man. Initiators say that boys need a second birth, this time a birth from men."[1]

- Robert Bly, *Iron John: A Book About Men*

WILD [ˈwi(-ə)ld] : adjective

1. intentionally deviating from the expected course
2. going beyond normal or conventional boundaries
3: passionately eager or enthusiastic

Foreword

There have been unique challenges in each generation. One point of confusion in our current culture has to do with what it means to be masculine. There is a difference between simply being male and being a man. One is predetermined genetically. The other is cultivated over time.

Zeke has properly identified a significant area of confusion in today's culture. What does it mean to be a man? Specifically, what does it mean to be a *Wild* man? How do we separate out the confusion of the culture and return to God's intent in making a child uniquely male, on purpose for a purpose?

The journey offered in *The Wild Man* fable and guidebook involves more than simply learning material in a book or classroom. It's a quest that older men can take with younger men to discover that part of themselves that is fearfully and wonderfully made by God.

This trek is not for the timid or faint of heart. It's an adventure for men of all ages, young and old, who want to be all that God created them to be.

Take this journey if you dare. You won't be disappointed.

Bryan Clark
Senior Pastor Emeritus, Lincoln Berean Church
Author of *God's Not Like That*

Preface

I spent an embarrassing amount of my childhood thinking about what toughness was and who most embodied it. I couldn't figure out how to get home by curfew or how to do simple math, but from fifth through twelfth grades, I could list in order the baddest dudes at school.

Looking back, I was trying to figure out who the men were so I could do whatever it took to join them. Who-could-beat-up-who was the low-hanging fruit, the easy-to-grab measurement of masculinity.

I didn't invent this measurement. It was given to the boys of my generation by our culture. I was seven when *Rocky* hit theaters, punching his way to the top of every man's toughness list. I went to the movie with my dad. We sat by several boys with their dads. You'd have thought we were watching a live boxing match. When the previously unknown Rocky Balboa stunned the reigning heavyweight champion Apollo Creed with his first punch, the theater turned into the Olympic Auditorium.

For nine years, I was certain Stallone was the manliest man alive. Then I saw Arnold Schwarzenegger in *Commando* in 1988, and I wasn't so sure. When Steven Seagal kicked tail and took names in *Above the Law*, I questioned all former conclusions. Who was the toughest, manliest man in the world? I wasn't sure ... until I met The Club in the summer of 1990.

A couple of weeks after my freshman year in college, our city-rec softball team went into a maximum-security facility to play the inmates. The men behind bars were solid

19

competition. They lifted weights every day and played ball most evenings. I manned third base that day. The first inning, the fourth man up for their team was an unusually large human being. The Louisville Slugger in his hands looked more like the miniature blue bat that I'd been given at a Royals' baseball game when I was ten years old. On the first pitch, he swung that bat as if it were weightless and the ball soared over right field, smacking the exterior fence and falling to the ground. The inmate rounded first, barreled past second, then dove head-first into third just as the cut-off man zipped the ball to me.

"I've never seen a ball go that far," I said.

"It come down yet?" he chuckled.

The man had a neck tattoo. The lines weren't crisp, which I found out later was due to how his roommate gave him the artwork using the motor from an electric toothbrush and the coiled spring from an ink pen. The tattoo pictured flames traveling upward from his shoulders to a spot behind his left ear. The clearest part of the tattoo was in the middle of the flames – it was the head of a golf club, a putter.

"You learn to swing like that on a golf course?" I asked, pointing at my neck, and then nodding toward his.

"Nah, I've only held a golf club once in my life," he said. "This one here on my neck."

The next guy up hit the ball over second base, and the man with a neck tattoo jogged home, touched the plate, and then circled back to his dugout for a series of high fives. The third base was only a few feet from the inmates' dugout. I heard one guy say, "Nice shot, Club." Another yelled, "Way to go, Clubber!"

The Club launched a few more satellites into orbit that game. When the game was over, the guards let us have a few minutes to talk with the inmates. Clubber walked up to me.

"Wanna hear the story?"

I really did.

He first told me about the crime that put him behind bars. The summer after high school, he and a friend had gotten high and tried to steal a car. While they were fishing a coat hanger through the window, the owner walked up. Clubber and his friend attacked him, sending him to the hospital. The Club was just nineteen years old when he was sentenced to five years at a medium-security facility in the Midwest.

"I'd gotten out ten years ago if I hadn't picked up this putter," he said. He paused, clearly for theatrics.

"When I first got in, I was scrawny. Tall, but no muscles. I was scared, everyone knew it."

He described how at dinner the first night, an inmate with tattoos over most of his face sat down at his table and put his thumb and index finger into the pressure points behind the young man's ears. "When he squeezed it felt like knives stabbing my brain," The Club said.

"He said, 'You're mine tonight. Be in the library at 7:00 or you won't live to see breakfast.'"

"What'd you do?" I gasped.

"I got this golf club from the rec center," he said, touching his neck again.

"They let you have golf clubs in here?" I asked.

"Not here, this was a different place. More relaxed. They had these green mats you could putt on if that was your thing."

Golf wasn't Clubber's thing. He had different plans. He took the putter to the library, arriving thirty minutes before 7:00. He hid in a closet just beyond the door. He waited. A minute or two after 7:00, the older inmate entered and walked past the closet. The Club swung the putter like a hatchet, bringing it down on the inmate's skull. The man dropped. When Clubber was sure he'd punched the guy's ticket, he left the library and gave the bloody club to a guard.

"They gave me life for that," he said with a smirk, "but nobody's messed with me since."

As I drove home from the game that afternoon, I couldn't quit thinking about The Club. I wanted the respect he had. Guards brought him bottles of water and told him he should be playing in the majors. His teammates gave him high-fives as if he were royalty. When The Club was up to bat, the inmates not playing in the game pressed against the fence to see how hard he'd hit the next pitch. I was impressed, maybe even envious.

How starved for vision does a young man need to be before he chooses a murderer serving a life sentence for his latest example of masculinity?

At nineteen, I was that hungry.

Six months after meeting The Club, God introduced me to Jesus through a couple of friends at college. One played football for Nebraska Wesleyan. I lifted weights, studied, and hunted with the other one. Both were strong and competitive, yet gentle and kind to others. They loved having fun, but were self-disciplined and did well in school. Perhaps what attracted me the most to these two friends was their willingness to talk about their failures. They were quicker to boast about their weaknesses than to talk about their strengths.

When I asked questions about what made them different, they pointed me to the grace and mercy of God through Christ. I'd never wanted anything to do with Christianity before my sophomore year in college, but the way my friends presented Jesus as a strong, courageous, other-centered Rescuer helped draw me to Christ.

On a Tuesday afternoon in November 1990, I got on my knees, and by God's grace, received forgiveness for my sins and the righteousness of Christ.

I also received a new vision of masculinity. As a new

Christian, the first book in the Bible I read was Luke's Gospel. Luke described how Jesus, from His gentle and lowly heart, was a fearless lover of people - *all people* - even the weak and marginalized. He didn't worry about popularity or public impressions. He was unafraid of the world's power structures. He was unselfconscious, comfortable in His skin. He was competent and wise.

Perhaps what most impressed me was how Jesus was a man on a mission. In chapter 9, verse 51, Luke records, "When the days drew near for him to be received up, he set his face to go to Jerusalem."

A lot of men set their faces on their strength, power, and glory, yet Jesus was determined to get to Jerusalem - His cross, grave, and resurrection - to defeat sin and death once and for all. Jesus' mission was to rescue helpless sinners and return to His Father. At the age of nineteen, I finally had a clear, perfect picture of masculinity to follow.

I wrote *The Wild Man* for my son Aidan to introduce him to the Wildest Man the world's ever known. I'm grateful for how God worked through my past and my wanderings, but **my hope is that my son, and your sons and grandsons, won't need to start from scratch. My prayer is that they won't adopt a warped view of manhood - too squishy, or too savage - from our present culture.**

I admit at the start, I'm not perfect. Far from it. I'm a man who needs to return to the grace and mercy of God every day for strength, vision, and my identity in Christ. I mention this in part so that you, the reader, won't feel the need to be perfect either. God's infinitely deep well of grace and mercy is new every morning for you just as it is for me.

Zeke Pipher
Central City, Nebraska
January 2024

The
Fable

1

n a land far beyond bubble baths and throw pillows lived a Wild Man. His hair was the rusty color of milo in autumn, and it sprouted proudly from every part of his body. He lived in a den carved into the face of the highest peak. Pebbles from the riverbed covered the floor, and a mink-lined hammock stretched from one side of the cave to the other.

Each morning, as the sun rose from behind the eastern hills, the Wild Man leaped from his den onto the Looking Rock. He scanned the valley below, selecting his prey from a variety of animals before charging down the mountain to hunt. The Wild Man pursued the healthiest of the herd. The chase thrilled him, and he believed that an animal's fitness would feed his own.

The Wild Man spent his afternoons enjoying his strength. He wrestled bears, pressed logs above his head, and threw boulders across the stream just to improve on yesterday's record. When the sun began to set, its golden beams struck the Wild Man's hair and made him look like a flash of fire as he raced up the mountain toward his den.

The village of Modernis was several valleys away from the Wild Mountain, and the people treasured the distance. Modernis was a tame and soft place. The men, clean-shaven and smelling of powders and perfumes, were gentle and pleasing to others. They played games, told jokes, and tried not to hurt one another's feelings. The women of Modernis were strong and assertive. They liked their men clean-shaven and their children close by.

The inhabitants of Modernis lived in constant terror of the Wild Man. Occasionally, the Wild Man let out a scream so fierce that it echoed throughout the canyon and turned the townsfolk's blood cold. These bellows signaled that the Wild Man was leaving his mountain to destroy flesh in the woods near Modernis, for in the days following a howl, villagers would find carcasses strewn about on the forest floor.

They also feared the Wild Man because the Wild Mountain seemed to gobble up boys from the villages nearby. Many decades ago, an adventurous young man from a neighboring town struck out toward the Wild Mountain, never to be seen again. Decades before his disappearance, as legend has it, another boy from a different village journeyed with his dog toward the Wild Mountain. Weeks later, the dog returned home without the young man. The pup's hair had turned white, and it never barked again. Something had scared the color from its coat and robbed the courage from its lungs.

The fear of the Wild Man made the townsfolk treasure the night's fog. Most evenings, as the air from the forest floor rose into the cool night, a soupy haze spread over Modernis like a protective shroud. The mist muffled the beast's howls and kept the townsfolk from having to see his fires. They were happy to trade a clear view for the foggy façade of security.

Occasionally, however, an evening breeze would sweep the mist down the valley, leaving Modernis exposed under a starry sky. Clear nights were dreadful nights. The community would huddle together in a dank cellar in the middle of town. As earthworms slithered over muddy toes, hands would beat the slop just to drown out the Wild Man's roar.

It was on one of those awfully clear nights that our story begins.

2

 here had been a thick murk over the village for most of the afternoon, but just as mothers were dishing up the evening pie, a wind whistled through the trees. Clear sky appeared.

Pie plates crashed to the floor. Men stopped talking in the middle of their jokes. The entire village ran toward the cellar. One by one, the villagers shuffled down the stairs and found their spots on the muddy ground. The candles lining the rocky walls illuminated the wide eyes of fearful people.

The slap of hands striking the mud continued for several hours and would have continued for many more if it hadn't been for the interruptive courage of a twelve-year-old boy. Shortly after midnight, Balen rose from his mother's side and stepped to the middle of the room.

Summoning his deepest voice, which wasn't very deep at all, he said, "I'm tired of being afraid! Someone must deal with the Wild Man once and for all."

The men shuffled backward, disappearing into the shadows of the cellar. The women shook their heads and gave disapproving looks.

Balen's mother stretched out her hand toward her son. Her eyes pleaded with him to return and sit back down by her side.

Balen considered remaining with his mother. She'd protected and nourished him for the first twelve years of his life. The boy loved his mother more than anyone in the world, but the heart in his chest burned like an ember from a fire.

He took her hand and helped her up off the floor. He hugged her, kissed her on the cheek, then said goodbye. He walked across the muddy floor toward the stairway.

The women turned toward the men in the shadows and gave them threatening looks. The men, fearing the women, but not enough to step out of the shadows, made a chorus of soft pleas to Balen.

"It's fine to do nothing," said one.

"Let's just survive the night," said another.

"You should always listen to your mother," one man suggested.

Balen stood on the first step. He tried to make out the faces of the men in the shadows. His heart ached to unite with the men of his village, but he couldn't even see them. They were veiled in darkness.

In a new, slightly deeper voice, Balen said, "I will climb the mountain and seize the Wild Man."

He climbed the steps, unlatched the iron bar on the cellar door, and stepped away from the tame and soft ways of his people.

When Balen barred the cellar door, he turned around. He froze in place, his eyes as wide as pancakes.

Standing before him was an Ancient Man, the likes of which Balen had never seen before. The elder had a dignified look of strength and wisdom. His eyes were the bluish-silver color of a storm cloud full of dynamic power. His skin was wrinkly, and the thick hair that covered his body was as white as freshly fallen snow. A long pipe hung casually from one side of his mouth.

"Beginning a quest, My Son?" the man asked, though in a way that sounded like he already knew the answer.

"Yes, Sir," Balen replied. "I'm going to capture the Wild Man."

"I'm proud of you," the Ancient Man said.

Balen had heard those words from his mother, but this was the first time a man had said them to him. The fire in his chest burn even hotter.

"For breaking from your village's soft and tame ways, receive this gift at the beginning of your journey."

The Ancient Man, with a quickness not expected, took a blade from his belt and slashed it toward Balen. A searing pain swept across the boy's torso. He fell backward onto the ground and looked up at the Ancient Man in shock. Then he looked at his body.

The Ancient Man had made a careful cut on the canvas of Balen's chest, ten inches long, from his left shoulder to the top of his right hip.

"Why?" the boy gasped.

The Ancient Man sheathed the blade and helped Balen up from the ground. He embraced the boy, pressing his tunic into the boy's wound.

The Ancient Man looked Balen in the eyes.

"I know your journey, Lad, and it's the noblest one. But there is a cost to what you seek.

This is the first of four marks you must receive before you can capture the Wild Man."

Though Balen's chest hurt, he took encouragement from the Ancient Man's words. He stumbled to the river by

33

the village gate to wash out the wound. When he returned, the Ancient Man was gone. The boy journeyed into the night, away from Modernis and toward the Wild Mountain.

3

ays, if not weeks, into the journey, Balen crossed a river he'd never seen before. When he emerged on the far bank, he sat down on a stump, took off his boots, and drained them of river water. Just then, a breeze carried a sweet, nutty aroma of pipe smoke to his nostrils. The boy looked up and saw the Ancient Man leaning against a tree.

"Certainly, you have time to help a family in need?" he asked the boy.

The Ancient Man took his pipe out of his mouth, and with the tip of the mouthpiece pointed toward a cabin on the far side of a vast field. Balen turned and saw a young woman on the porch nursing a newborn baby. Her husband was sitting by her side. He had a splint and a bandage running the full length of his right leg.

"If they don't clear this field of boulders, they'll never get a crop planted this year," the Ancient Man said, now pointing the mouthpiece of his pipe toward the large pasture filled with watermelon-sized stones.

Balen studied the field. It would take him weeks, if not months, to move the rocks. He wasn't even sure if he was strong enough to do it. What's more, he was already occupied with the noble task of journeying toward the Wild Mountain. He was about to say no, but when he looked at the family on the porch once more, he felt that same burning in his chest that had compelled him to take this journey in the first place. He knew he must help.

Balen took off his tunic and, with great effort, hoisted the first boulder onto his shoulder and carried it to the edge of the field. Then the second. Then the third.

For many weeks, if not months, Balen labored to clear that field. With every stone he moved, he felt the muscles in his body waking up and gaining strength. Blisters turned to callouses as the work turned into pleasure. With each new day, Balen found more delight in his strength. Eventually, Balen made a game of it, throwing the stones toward the outer edge, just to see if he could beat his previous record.

On the final day, an older and stronger Balen, with only one hand mind you, hoisted the last, and largest boulder above his head effortlessly. His young legs which had looked like corn stalks when he'd begun, were now thick and strong. They carried him across the field with ease.

As he set the last stone into place in the rock wall, Balen noticed prickly hair sprouting from his forearms. He rubbed his cheeks to find that they, too, had scratchy stubble. The hair was short, but it was colorful and promising.

Just then, Balen felt a tap on his shoulder. He turned around to find the Ancient Man standing close to him, the blade in his hand once again.

"You helped this family well. For your service, allow me to give you your second gift."

The blade slashing through the air caught a beam from the sun and almost seemed to glow with glory as it cut a second mark on Balen's chest. This one traveled from his right shoulder to his left hip. The marks combined to make a crooked "X" on his chest.

"Once again, I'm proud of you," the Ancient Man said, hugging the young man, beard on beard, now that Balen had hair emerging from his cheeks.

After sharing a meal of venison stew, the two said goodbye. Balen resumed his journey toward the Wild Mountain.

4

 fter traveling several days, if not weeks, Balen rounded a bend near the top of a hill and heard whistling coming from someplace below. Down the hill, he saw two brightly dressed travelers dancing arm in arm in a clearing in a shady valley.

The spinning companions were laughing and having a jolly good time. Balen was captivated by the bright and shiny colors and his heart raced with the hope of pleasant company. He left the high road and scampered down the path toward the valley below.

When he reached the two curious figures, he noticed that their costumes were extremely different from one another. The first dancer, a girl, or possibly a boy – Balen couldn't tell – wore very little clothing, and what she, or he, wore was silky and thin. At first glance, Balen felt embarrassed for the Seductive Stranger. He wondered if she, or he, knew how much of her, or his, body was visible.

At second glance, Balen felt embarrassed for himself. Shame pulsed through his veins. He stared at the grass between his feet.

The dancer slipped closer. Balen lifted his head and looked at the figure who was now standing uncomfortably close to him. The Seductive Stranger's eyes glinted like the sharp end of a sword.

"I know you desire to look at me. Go ahead. I'm a delicious feast for your eyes," she, or he, sang in a promising tone.

The urge to look at the Seductive Stranger felt almost irresistible. Balen raised his head, but as he did, he caught a glimpse of something terrifying. Behind the Seductive Stranger, in her, or his shadow, were dozens of men and boys slumped against trees. At first, Balen couldn't tell whether the men were alive or not. They were all gazing upon the Seductive Stranger, but with eyes revealing the dull transparency of the almost dead.

One of the sagging souls closest to Balen briefly pulled his eyes away from the Seductive Stranger to look toward the boy. When their eyes met Balen's, the man ever so slightly shook his head as if to warn Balen away from something. An instant later, however, the man swung his head back so he could gaze upon the Seductive Stranger once again.

Balen recognized the lie. The Seductive Stranger wasn't offering him pleasure or life. The feast she, or he, promised had Balen's own heart on the menu. He turned away.

As he did, the second traveler danced up to him, and in a playful tone, said, "This is a heavy life, but I can take your mind off your worries!"

Balen was once again captivated by the fascinating attire. The Foolishly Fun Stranger twirled around with his arms and legs out to his side, showing Balen that every toy a young man could ever want to play with hung from his cloak—cards and marbles, bows and arrows, fishing poles and slingshots—he offered it all.

"The best life is the one lived in play," the dancer declared to Balen.

Once again, Balen felt a strong desire to take up the stranger's invitation. His eyes widened as he watched the various playthings flash in front of his face. For several minutes, if not hours, the boy forgot the promise he'd made to his village. He forgot about the satisfaction of clearing boulders for the family in need. He forgot about how good it had felt to receive the approval of the Ancient Man. Indeed, Balen forgot about all things important.

As Balen stepped closer to inspect a toy of particular interest, he noticed that this stranger also had a long, dark shadow. Like the Seductive Stranger, the darkness behind the Foolishly Fun Stranger was littered with countless men and boys, each with a stack of games and toys beside them. They were in continuous motion, setting one down to pick another one up, over and over again. Like those in the wake of the Seductive Stranger, these men and boys barely looked alive.

The playthings that moments earlier seemed so inviting now felt threatening. Everything about the Shady Valley felt eerie to Balen. It was then that the young man remembered his promise and mission. He raced up the hill and back onto the path.

The light of the sun struck his body with warmth and illuminated the hair on his arms and legs, hair that had grown a bit longer as he exited the lowlands.

5

 uite a ways down the path, as the young man hopped from rock to rock along a riverbank, he heard the screams of children. He left the creek and ran through the trees in the direction of the cries. Pushing through a thicket, Balen popped out into a meadow.

In the middle of the field, pacing back and forth in a frightful manner was a bear, thick and brutish. It's claws ripped up chunks of sod as the slobber of hunger dripped from its teeth.

Beyond the bear, three children huddled together crying. They were trapped against a thorny shrub with nowhere to run.

Balen froze in his tracks. Growing up in the soft and tame village of Modernis, he'd never learned to fight or hunt. The men hadn't taught him how to run toward danger, only how to hide from it. For a moment, Balen considered shuffling backward and disappearing in the shadows as the men in his village had done that night in the cellar. Just then, a familiar sweet and nutty smell of pipe smoke swept across the wind and entered his nostrils.

Balen glanced to the side and saw the Ancient Man sitting on a stump a few yards away.

"Surely you have time to rescue the weak from the strong?" he asked, pointing the tip of his pipe toward the children and the bear.

Balen noticed the blade that hung from the Ancient Man's side. He touched the two wounds on his chest, both now closed and healed. They felt like symbols of courage and sacrifice, and they reminded Balen of how good it feels to do the right thing.

Balen looked back at the meadow. The creature was now popping its jaws as bears do before they charge. The white-hot ember once again burned in his heart, and Balen exploded toward the bear, like an arrow shot from a bow.

The bear stood up on its back legs and roared. Balen lunged at the brute and the two met in a violent clutch. They wrestled and fought for hours, if not days, exchanging blows and positions of strength. As the match continued, the bear tired, but Balen found new muscles and stamina. He developed new skills and techniques throughout the match, eventually putting the bear in a headlock so tight, it put the beast to sleep.

As Balen released his grasp and pulled his arm from around the bear's neck, he noticed the hairs on his hand and arm had grown thicker; they were nearly as long as the bear's fur. He ran to the river and splashed cold water upon his face and neck. When the ripples cleared, Balen gazed upon his reflection. He looked older. His eyes seemed bluer than he'd remembered, and the hair now sprouting proudly on his head and neck seemed darker and redder than ever before.

He stood up and turned around. The Ancient Man

approached Balen with his blade in his hand.

"For rescuing the weak from the strong, receive your third mark."

This third cut ran down the center of Balen's chest in a straight line, intersecting with the "X" precisely at the junction where the first two marks connected.

The Ancient Man expressed his respect for Balen. He hugged him and blessed him against all upcoming trials. The young man felt more alive than ever before.

Moments later, Balen collapsed into a hero's sleep, resting his head on the bear's neck as a pillow.

When he awoke, he resumed his journey toward the Wild Mountain, stopping frequently at rivers and streams to remove his tunic and soothe his third mark in the healing waters.

6

 or the final stretch of the journey, which lasted months, if not years, the Ancient Man traveled with Balen. The old taught the young how to build shelters and smokehouses, which plants were good for food, and how to make fires for warmth and cooking. The Ancient Man taught Balen how to hunt and fish, and the value of selecting the strongest of the herd to pursue.

"The health of the animal will feed your own," he'd say to the young man.

Through stories, lessons, challenges, and chores the Ancient Man opened the multifaceted, verdant world of masculinity to Balen. The more the young man lived in this new world, the more the rust-orange-colored hair on his head, face, and body grew long and thick. What had started as a peachy fuzz at the beginning of the journey was quickly developing into a lion's mane around Balen's face.

Many nights, after an honest day's work together,

Balen and the Ancient Man would sit by the fire, laughing, talking, and rubbing their beards like two old friends. Which, of course, they'd become.

Yet, on the last day of the trek, as the two neared the Wild Mountain, the Ancient Man turned to Balen, and said, "I must leave you to earn your final mark."

Balen stood alone at the base of the mountain. He felt smaller than he'd ever felt before. The massive alp rising before him was wider and higher than it appeared from the cobblestone streets of Modernis.

The sun was setting, and the night's shadow was creeping across the land and darkening the path up the mountain. Balen looked up and saw in the distance the Wild Man's ferocious fire. He felt even smaller, for the blaze also appeared much larger from the base of the Wild Mountain than it had from the safety of his village.

A long-forgotten fear crept back into Balen's heart – the terror he'd once shared with his villagers toward the unknown creature at the top of the Wild Mountain.

"What if the Wild Man, like the mountain and the fire, is even more ferocious and large in person," Balen wondered.

That idea made his blood turn cold. It also made his legs feel like they were stuck in quicksand. It was a long way up and he knew he should start climbing, but he couldn't bring himself to take a step.

The young man sat down on a watermelon-sized rock, much like the ones he moved from the field when his journey first began. He remembered the thrill of serving that family in need. That memory reminded him of the pleasure of receiving the second mark and the approval of the Ancient Man. Then he recalled the joy in saving the children by wrestling the bear.

As Balen remembered every part of his journey, as well as his concern for his mother and village, the heart within his chest once again became hot like an ember from a fire. His legs no longer seemed trapped in quicksand. Balen stood up and took a step. Then another.

With each stride up the Wild Mountain, Balen felt new muscles—mountain climbing muscles—waking up and gaining strength. Before long, he was jumping from boulder to boulder, racing up the mountain. As he neared the top, the golden-red beams from the Wild Man's blaze struck Balen's body and made him look like a flash of fire ascending the peak.

With a final bound, Balen jumped from a large boulder and landed on the Looking Rock.

He summoned his deepest voice, which was quite deep by now, and let out a roar.

Ready to seize the unfamiliar creature beside the fire, he turned toward the Wild Man.

Their eyes met.

Balen gasped. His knees buckled in shock.

7

 alen had prepared himself to see something unfamiliar. Yet, the Wild Man staring back at him was anything but foreign. He didn't look strange, at all. He looked *like Balen*.

The Wild Man was older, of course. His hair, once the rusty color of milo in autumn now bore hints of gray and white. He had wrinkles on the skin between his eyes and beard. But beyond signs of age, the two men standing before one another at the peak of the Wild Mountain were more alike than different. They were cut from the same cloth.

The Wild Man stood up straight with his shoulders back, showing Balen his chest. Balen's knees buckled once more. Beneath the tangle of hair on his chest, the Wild Man bore the same markings that the Ancient Man had given Balen. Only, Balen noticed, the Wild Man had an additional scar, which the boy surmised must be the fourth and final mark.

Whatever remaining fear Balen carried up the mountain fled when the Wild Man smiled. At that moment, he reminded Balen of the Ancient Man, for it was the same approving smile Balen had enjoyed many times before.

Just then, the Ancient Man walked around a boulder and into the light of the fire. He was wearing one of those approving smiles on his face.

The Ancient Man moved toward the two men, embracing them both at the same time.

He let go, stepped back, and then motioned for the Wild Man and Balen to join him beside the fire. The three men moved toward the blaze.

The Ancient Man looked at the Wild Man as if to invite his agreement. The Wild Man smiled again and nodded his head. The Ancient Man removed the blade from his side and set it onto the fire stone so that the flames kissed the tip of the knife. When the point was red hot, he retrieved it.

The Ancient Man and the Wild Man stood shoulder to shoulder before Balen. Balen's heart pounded like a tribal drum. He knew what was coming. He'd been longing for this moment for months, if not years. He stood up straight with his shoulders back. He kept his eyes open, not wanting to miss a thing.

The Ancient Man said to Balen, "For facing your fears in order to seize what is wild, receive your final mark."

The blade sliced through the crisp night air, this time in an arcing motion, cutting a gash in the form of a half-circle at the top of Balen's chest. The four marks combined to form the Ancient Symbol of Deep Masculinity.

The Ancient Man removed his tunic, revealing that he also bore the marks. All three men shared the symbol.

The only remaining step in the initiation was to change Balen's name, for as you may know, the name "Balen" means "youthful boy."

That label no longer fit the lion-hearted man standing atop the Wild Mountain.

"From now on, you shall be called 'Aidan, the Ancient Man declared, "for the fire in your chest has made you a man!"

The three men threw their hands to the skies, and with armored hearts, roared, simply for the pleasure of roaring together.

8

 or decades, if not centuries, the three Wild Men enjoyed the warmest friendships that creation has ever known. The Tribe spent their days hunting, fishing, wrestling bears, and pressing logs above their heads. In work or play, they celebrated each other's strengths and made up for each other's weaknesses.

They did all of this, of course, when they weren't rescuing people. To be Wild is to protect everyone in the land, even those who fear your existence.

The three men took turns each night on the Looking Rock, guarding the citizens of Modernis and the other villages in the valley. If they spotted a pack of marauders or wild beasts getting too close to a town, they'd let out a ferocious roar before descending the mountain to fight. Many a menacing creature met its end in the dark forests surrounding Modernis; its bones, strewn about the forest floor, served as a sign of the watchful eyes of the Wild Men.

From those days forward, and even up to this very one in which you are holding this book, the Tribe of Wild Men has continued to grow. Not quickly, or by great numbers, mind you. Most boys have a hard time leaving the land of bubble baths and throw pillows.

But those who do have entered into the deeper thrills of being Wild. They have found their voices and learned to roar.

The
Guidebook

A Chance to Bleed

In his book, *Iron John*, Robert Bly describes the ancient process of initiation into manhood employed by the Kikuyu tribe in Kenya. When a boy was ready to become a man, the adult men in the tribe took him away from the village—away from his mother, sisters, and all the other comforts of his boyhood world—and they lead him to a sacred place where only the men go. They required the boy to fast for three days, and then on the third night, they joined him around a campfire—a tribe of elders and an extremely hungry young man.

The initiation began when one of the older men took a ceremonial knife and opened a vein in his own arm. He collected some of his blood in a gourd and passed the knife and gourd to the next man. That man took the knife and did the same thing. The cutting and the collecting continued until each adult male in the tribe had contributed to the bowl. At that point, the bowl was passed to the boy, and he was invited to satisfy his hunger by drinking from the gourd.

That may sound gruesome to our "civilized" minds, but the young man learned several valuable lessons through this ceremony. He discovered that his elders took seriously their responsibility to pass on masculinity; so seriously, they were willing to bleed for it. He learned that only men could initiate boys into manhood. He saw that a knife could be used for deep and wholesome purposes, and not merely for playing or fighting.

Importantly, he gained a picture of how blood represented the life of another person and how, through the blood of his male elders, he had been invited into the life of the men in his tribe.

This entire ritual gave the Kikuyu boys the chance to explore, understand, and feel invited into the world of Manhood. Manhood and Womanhood are two different worlds - equally vital and honorable - but yet different. The Kikuyu tribe knew that boys needed to break away from the world of Womanhood for a time, as Sam Keen writes in *Fire in the Belly*:

> "Premodern societies knew the overwhelming power of woman and that boys could only emerge into manhood if they separated from her and entered for a time into an all-male world. Male rites of passage were designed to allow boys to escape from woman's world long enough to discover the shape of man's world. They knew that men must resist the danger of being defined by women (and vice versa). The sexes were pried apart and isolated to explore their separate truths before they could come together."[2]

This guidebook provides older men a map they can use in leading boys into the world of Manhood. It gives them a chance to bleed - open their hearts, minds, and histories – and give themselves to the next generation of boys and men.

A Word on Masculinity

 In *The Wild Man* fable, the Ancient Symbol of Deep Masculinity is simply the Chi-Rho image representing Christ. Chi is the first Greek letter in "Christ," and Rho is the second. I chose this symbol because all the positive qualities and virtues described in the fable are perfectly revealed to us in the person and work of Jesus. He is our Provider, Keeper, and Rescuer. He is also the One who transforms us by His Spirit into the men we long to be.

I also chose this symbol because **boys and men only become Wild when they seek Christ first, and masculinity second.** This is a subtle, but critical distinction. A boy or man who seeks masculinity for its own sake will become self-absorbed and savage. His "masculinity project" will be fueled by self, and anything fueled by self becomes selfish.

But the boy or man who pursues Christ above all things will be motivated by grace and mercy. He will pursue masculinity for the glory of God and for the purpose of serving others as God in Christ has served him. He will enjoy and employ whatever masculine strength and competence God gives him in love for his Father in heaven, not in love for self or the things of this world, as the Apostle John commands:

> "I write to you, young men, because you are strong, and the word of God abides in you, and you have overcome the evil one. Do not love the world or the things in the world. If anyone loves the world, the

love of the Father is not in him."[3]

Fables use symbols to make abstract ideas concrete. In *The Wild Man* masculinity is represented by hair and physical strength. However, you do not need to have a beard or large biceps to be masculine. Many of the young men who go through this material are years away from being able to grow facial hair or lift impressive weights. Likewise, many of the older men who read this book have lost their hair and many of the physical abilities of their youth. Neither situation limits a man's opportunity to be wild.

Many today reduce the definition of masculinity down to haircuts, clothing styles, risky stunts, and physical abilities. This narrow, external-focused picture of masculinity pushes many of our most masculine men out of the category. That is a sad, unnecessary loss.

To be masculine is to carry the right vision and do the right things because you follow the right King. It's to have a heart that - because it has found freedom in the grace and mercy of Christ - is other-centered and focused on loving, providing, protecting, and serving everyone in our care. Being masculine does often involve being strong, but God designed masculine strength to take many forms.

The fraternity of wild men is varied, abundant, and multi-sided. You will find that it has plenty of room for your style, abilities, personality, interests, weaknesses, and strengths.

How to Begin

1. FORM a tribe of friends and family. (Make sure each member of your tribe has a copy of The Wild Man.)

A "tribe" is simply a group of companions or family members that shares the same customs, convictions, values, and history. The first step in this 14-week adventure involves inviting a small group of men to be a part of your tribe. Your tribe will consist of a few older men (fathers, grandfathers, and mentors) and a few younger men (sons, grandsons, and young men in need of father-figures). Some tribes will consist of a few fathers and a few sons, but not all tribes will look this way.

All young men need wisdom and vision from older men, and sometimes the older men are active, engaged fathers. But sadly, this isn't always possible. When a father-son teaching relationship isn't possible, it falls to grandfathers, uncles, or other father-figures to hand on a vision for masculinity.

This fable and guidebook present a journey for all men who want to cast a vision for what it looks like to live a truly masculine—truly wild—life as a man of God.

As you gather a tribe, keep in mind the main two objectives for this journey:

A. To help men hold important discussions about masculinity.

This book will raise far more questions than it will answer. This book isn't aiming to resolve all issues concerning masculinity; but it will help men have important discussions with people they love.

B. To help men—young and old—develop strong, supportive friendships.

We all desire to have brother-to-brother relationships, but only men striving toward the same vision find it.

CS Lewis writes: "The very condition of having Friends is that we should want something else besides friends... Those who have nothing can share nothing; those who are going nowhere can have no fellow-travellers."[4]

The Wild Man fable and guidebook gives men a chance to go somewhere together.

2. READ The Wild Man fable at the beginning of this book before starting the 14 weeks.

Why begin with a fable? Because we need vision. "Where there is no vision, the people are unrestrained."[5]

Nothing holds the power to direct our lives like the tales we tell. Fables remind us of what we want, and what is possible. G.K. Chesterton writes about bogey, the imaginary evil character that carries off naughty children:

"Fairy tales do not give the child his first idea of bogey. What fairy tales give the child is his first clear idea of the possibility of defeat of bogey."[6]

The Wild Man fable illuminates some of our culture's most threatening bogeymen and shows men—young and old—that together, with the Lord's help, they can be killed.

Many of the phrases and ideas used in the 14-week guidebook have been taken directly from *The Wild Man* fable, so it is important to have everyone read it before taking the journey.

3. SELECT a sacred space for your tribe to meet.

Rooms, structures, and spaces communicate vision to us, telling us what to expect while we are inside. For example, when you enter a comfortable living room, you sense it's a place to relax and let your guard down. Conversely, when you enter a cold, marble-floored structure, you sense formality and tradition. A football stadium tells us we're free to yell and have fun. A library whispers to us that we'd better stay quiet.

These tribal discussions are unique, so hold them someplace out of the ordinary. Consider meeting in the corner of an old barn, a sportsman's club, a workshop, or around a firepit.

4. MEET with your tribe once a week for 14-weeks.

Plan to meet as a tribe each week for about 60-90 minutes. Each tribal discussion involves reading a few thoughts at the beginning of the section, and then having a discussion together based on the questions provided. There will be a time for prayer at the end of each discussion.

5. PERSONALIZE your adventure.

This is *your* journey with *your* tribe, so find ways to personalize this adventure and make it exciting. Consider having the older men go fourteen weeks without shaving. Perhaps design hats, shirts, or jackets with a logo that you have designed for your particular Tribe.

You may want to add additional Scripture memory

challenges, service projects, or team-work exercises to your journey. Have fun, be creative, and make the most of these fourteen weeks together.

6. FEAST and INITIATE.

At the end of the 14-weeks, the older men should plan a Wild Mountain Feast to celebrate the conclusion of this journey. If the boys are old enough for initiation into manhood, come up with a creative way to celebrate and initiate the young men into the ancient fraternity of wild masculinity.

The Facilitator's Role

1. **DIRECT the process of forming a tribe:** Someone needs to invite men into a tribe, and this is often the role of the facilitator. A tribe might consist of two dads and two sons, or it could contain any combination of grandfathers, fathers, sons, father-figures, and young men who need father-figures. To have good interactions each week, the ideal size for a tribe is between 6-12 participants.

2. **HOST a get-together for the fathers, grandfathers, and mentors prior to the 14-week study with the young men:** Before a tribe begins their 14-week journey, the facilitator might consider calling the older men in each tribe to meet once to set a vision for your times together, praying for the upcoming discussions.

   Many older men will feel challenged, or even intimidated, by this journey toward masculinity. That's perfectly normal, and the facilitator can use this initial meeting to help each man see that he's in good company.

3. **CREATE a safe environment:** The facilitator doesn't need to lead every meeting, but he will be responsible for inviting men—young and old—into the tribe, and for setting the tone of the group.

   The facilitator is primarily responsible for helping each man—young and old—find a chance to speak, and a chance to listen. The facilitator should regularly remind the group that the discussions that happen within a tribe are confidential. Trust is vital for a tribe to develop strong relationships and move closer to the Wild Mountain.

Occasionally, a facilitator may need to tactfully encourage one of the tribal members to speak less and listen more. There's a convicting line from a Robert Bly poem that I think of often; it cautions me when I'm in a group discussion. Bly writes,

> "I can't be the noisy person I am
> If you don't stop talking."[7]

Facilitator's need to be courageous and kind as they encourage some to talk more, and some to talk less.

4. **POINT men back to Jesus**: The facilitator doesn't need to solve his tribe member's problems or have vast insights into the topics that will be discussed. The facilitator is merely responsible for making sure that every person in the tribe feels welcomed and valued, and that everyone gets a chance to speak and respond to others.

God, through the help of the Holy Spirit, in the context of strong relationships, will encourage, inspire, and renew men during this journey to the Wild Mountain.

The weight of healing men's hearts and inspiring them to be wild is not on the facilitator's shoulders. It's on the Lord's, and He is strong, able, and always faithful.

Note for Pastors and Ministry Leaders

This fable and guidebook were designed in part to be used by churches, college ministries, parachurch organizations, and various other men's groups. If you are considering forming tribes from your community, it might be a good idea to hold a pre-meeting (Tribal Council of Ancients) for the fathers/father-figures in the group.

Many of the discussions that men will have together on this journey will be challenging. Some men will be asked to verbalize thoughts and feelings they have never spoken aloud before or will be encouraged to engage their sons and grandsons in new ways. For these reasons, it might be helpful for a pastor or leader to address the older men before the 14-week journey begins to communicate a few important ideas, such as:

You are free to share with your tribe as much as you'd like, but you are not under any pressure to divulge information. These tribal discussions must not pressure or manipulate anyone into saying something they might regret later. Part of building trust with one another involves allowing each man to freely choose what he is comfortable sharing with his tribe.

No one person should dominate a tribe's discussions. The goal for these tribal discussions is to hear from everyone, and so it's important that each participant focuses as much attention to listening as they do to talking.

These discussions will surface issues and memories that are sometimes painful. We all have regrets, and we all have sin in our lives that we wish we could get rid of. It's important for men to know that they're not alone in feeling regret or conviction of sin, and that there is grace and forgiveness for absolutely every issue that might surface on the journey toward the Wild Mountain.

Many men—young and old—are longing for a father-figure or mentor, but they haven't had that need met by their biological fathers. This journey is designed so that any mature older man could step into that father-figure role.

14 Week Journey

Week 1

Wild Versus Savage

Read Aloud

"The true power that is available to us, the power that multiplies power, lies on the other side of the choice to empty ourselves of power." – Andy Crouch, *Playing God*[8]

"True manhood, to Jonathan Edwards, isn't a hard, tough exterior with a soft, spineless interior, but just the opposite—a steely, rock-solid interior mediated through an exterior emanating with the beauty of gentleness. Manliness isn't machismo. Masculinity isn't inadequacy-mitigating posturing and chest-puffing. On the other hand, gentleness isn't cowardice. Both non-gentle masculinity and also non-manly gentleness are to be avoided." - Dane Ortlund[9]

"He has told you, O man, what is good; and what does the LORD require of you but to do justice, and to love kindness, and to walk humbly with your God?" – Micah 6:8, ESV

The Westminster Shorter Catechism asks the question, "What is the chief end of man?"

It answers, "Man's chief end is to glorify God, and to enjoy Him forever."

A savage man exists to promote himself and enjoy his

power and influence for his own sake. Savage men are prideful about their masculinity and use their strength—voices, bodies, or positions—to dominate others. For this reason, a savage man's power is something others fear, and for good reasons; savage men are known to abuse and hurt other people in their aggressive pursuit of ego. Even a Christian man can be a savage man if he carries a warped view of masculinity.

In contrast, wild men are powerful, and at times fierce, but they are always self-controlled and focused on the welfare of others. The wild man's power has been transformed by the love of God. He no longer lives for his glory and reputation; he now exists to care for others with the unselfish and sacrificial concern that God has shown him.

Wild men are something to behold today, a rare sight. At the center of their hearts, wild men carry a white-hot ember that burns for the glory of God. This ember is hotter than the flames of hell, and it fuels wild men's passion for caring for others.

Our culture presents several confusing, and often conflicting, definitions of masculinity. Through video games, violent movies, ego-filled sports stars, and power-hungry politicians, young men experience thousands of images and examples of savage men each week. This is not healthy. This does not help young men form a vision for becoming strong, ego-less, responsible men.

As older men, we must present a different vision to our sons, grandsons, and other young men in our community—living examples of how rich, varied, and flourishing masculinity can be. That is precisely what we will do over the next fourteen weeks. We will grow wilder. Together.

For Discussion

1. In The Wild Man fable, how did the Wild Man and the Ancient Man display power? Did their power benefit others or

harm others?

2. Can you think of one time recently that you used your power to serve or protect others?

3. Can you think of one time recently when you selfishly used your strength and power to intimidate someone or get your way?

4. When you think about our culture—celebrities, political leaders, athletes, and artists—how do you think our society defines masculinity?

5. What do you agree with, or disagree with, about our culture's definition of masculinity?

6. Can you think of a man in your life who seems to be faithfully living out Micah 6:8 by doing justice, loving kindness, and walking humbly with his God? Describe him.

Prayer

Have one of the older men in your tribe read 1 Timothy 4:8.

Close in prayer, asking God to give each man a vision of being a faithful, masculine, truly wild man.

Challenge for the Week

Do one thing each day this week to serve someone else. For example, consider doing a sibling's chores for him/her, washing the dishes for your wife, or mowing your neighbor's lawn. Choose one simple, practical way to use your strength to be kind to someone each day this week.

Week 2

Father-Hunger

Read Aloud

> When the father-table, the groundwater, drops, so to speak, and there is too little father, instead of too much father, the sons find themselves in a new situation. What do they do: drill for new father water, ration the father water, hoard it, distill mother water into father water? – Robert Bly, *Iron John*[10]

> "Fathers represent God in the home in many ways...
> ...Done correctly, the child feels loved, valued, and secure at home. Done poorly, the father wound often leads to rebellion with the children that will hinder any kind of meaningful relationship with the heavenly Father." – Bryan Clark, *God's Not Like That*[11]

> "Brothers, join in imitating me, and keep your eyes on those who walk according to the example you have in us." –Philippians 3:17, ESV

All of us are born with a hunger for a father. Just as our bodies need salt, water, and various nutrients, a boy's heart craves a father's love. This means that a father, or father figure, is the only one who can satisfy this specific longing. This reality doesn't diminish the contribution or value of mothers, yet as hard as mothers may try, they cannot impart what only fathers were designed to provide.

This father-hunger creates two realities. First, with such an intense appetite comes a great potential for hunger pangs. Indeed, many of us live with father-wounds because our longings for our dads weren't satisfied. A second reality created by this need involves our expectations; precisely because we carry such weighty hopes for our fathers, our dads are bound to fail us. Most fathers carry a strong desire to meet their son's needs, and yet they see the disappointment in their son's eyes for not quite measuring up.

These two difficult realities caused by our father-hunger lead us to two important truths as we journey to the Wild Mountain:

1. First, we need to show each other grace.

As we journey toward the Wild Mountain together, we must try to understand one another. We must imagine one another's experiences of life and allow that imagination to create empathy and compassion in our hearts. Moral imagination is not always easy, or instinctive, but it is an essential part of becoming a truly wild, masculine man.

As we consider each other, we will find many opportunities to ask for forgiveness, grant forgiveness, and receive forgiveness. This will likely be a difficult part of the adventure. Some of us have been deeply wounded by our father's anger, abuse, and addictions. Some of us have been hurt by our sons. There is no way to sugar-coat the reality that the journey toward masculinity is hard. It requires us to tap into the deep vein of God's grace and mercy toward us so that we might show that same grace and mercy to each other. There is no other way to reach the Wild Mountain. We must come to terms with the fact that however difficult, the path of grace and mercy is the only one that moves us forward.

2. Secondly, men need to look to their Father in Heaven to meet their deepest father-hunger.

It's important to see that our father-hunger and wounds present tremendous opportunities to find deep satisfaction in our relationship with our Father in Heaven. All of us—as grandfathers, fathers, sons, and the fatherless—can cry out, "Abba! Father!" from our hearts because we have found what we crave most deeply in God as our Father.

The beauty of this is that the more we see God meet our father-hunger, the more grace and mercy we can show to our fathers on earth. When God is our Father, we can finally stop expecting the impossible from our flawed, finite fathers on earth. This frees us to be wild as sons. This frees us to be wild as fathers. And this frees us to be wild as a Tribe of less-than-perfect people.

For Discussion

1. From last week's Challenge for the Week: Describe a couple of opportunities God gave you last week to use your power to be kind to, or sacrifice for, someone.

2. What is a quality or attribute that you admire about your father or the primary father figure in your life? If possible, describe a memory of your father that helps you demonstrate that quality or attribute.

3. For the older men to answer: When you think about yourself as a father or father figure what is one thing that you wish you did better or had done differently?

4. In Romans 8:15, Paul tells us that the Spirit of God gives a person of faith a sense of sonship. Paul writes, "...but you have received the Spirit of adoption as sons, by whom we cry, 'Abba! Father!'"

Do you find it hard or easy to think about God as your Father? Explain why.

5. In *The Wild Man* fable, Balen needed to find men beyond his family and village to show him what a father's love looks like. Describe one person, other than your father, who has helped you understand the idea of fatherly love.

Pray

Have one of the older men read Romans 8:12-17.

Close in prayer, asking God to give each man in your tribe a heart that can sincerely cry out, "Abba! Father!"

Challenge for the Week

The challenge for this week is to write a short letter to your father, or a father figure, telling him a few things you admire about him.

Week 3

What Makes a Man Measure Up?

Read Aloud

"Nobody's ever gone the distance with Creed, and if I can go that distance, you see, and that bell rings and I'm still standin', I'm gonna know for the first time in my life, see, that I weren't just another bum from the neighborhood." – Rocky Balboa, *Rocky*

"For our sake he made him to be sin who knew no sin, so that in him we might become the righteousness of God." – 2 Corinthians 5:21, ESV

"And to the one who does not work but trusts him who justifies the ungodly, his faith is counted as righteousness..." – Romans 4:5, ESV

In the movie, *Rocky*, the main character, Rocky Balboa, is driven to prove he could measure up by achieving great things. The movie was a hit because we could all relate to his pressure to perform.

I was ten years old when I first watched *Rocky*. When the movie ended, I cracked two eggs into a drinking glass like Rocky had, gagged a little as I swallowed them, and then did ten pushups on the red shag carpet in my bedroom. As I stood in front of my mirror, flexing the non-existent muscles on my stringy arms, I thought, "I don't want to be just another bum from the neighborhood either."

This performance-oriented way of life began the moment Adam and Eve lost their relationship with God.

Before sin uprooted them from their Creator, they didn't question their significance. But with sin, all humanity lost their relationship to their Source of life and acceptance. Yet, no one can live without significance and acceptance, so where do we turn when we can no longer turn to God?

The only place we know to look is to ourselves. We look to our accomplishments, results, and performance to try to feel worthy or acceptable.

Many of us men believe the lie that we are just a few major accomplishments from finally proving to ourselves that we measure up. So, we keep striving, focusing on our work, honing our performance, and anxiously weighing the results. This will never work, and deep inside, if we're honest, we know this is true. Enough will never be enough, no matter how great the results. Rocky illustrates this point. The Italian Stallion did go twelve rounds with Apollo Creed. Thousands of people cheered him on as he became Philadelphia's favorite son. The city made a statue of him. But, did these things finally prove to Rocky that he wasn't a bum?

The fact that we have another five Rocky movies suggests that they didn't. That same angst of unfinished work shows up in every movie that follows. The Italian Stallion kept knocking down enemies and breaking through barriers. He kept producing bigger and better results, yet he never found rest.

The only way for us to find rest and know once and for all that we measure up is by applying and appropriating the grace of God into every aspect of life. Faith in Jesus is trusting that the work is done. Jesus did it. The man of God could never be "just another bum from the neighborhood." Through faith, he is the "righteousness of God (2 Cor. 5:21b)."

My friend Bryan Clark asks the right questions in his book, *God's Not Like That*:

"How many Christians will spend a lifetime trying to prove they have value... to people who don't really care? How many will agonize to gain favor from a God who already loves them, accepts them, and celebrates them in Christ?"[12]

For Discussion

1. Rocky tried to find his significance and acceptance by gaining success in the boxing ring. What are the achievements and accomplishments (i.e. titles, awards, abilities, earnings, etc.) that you tend to look to feel significant and acceptable?

2. Have someone read Romans 3:21-26.

What makes a man righteous, significant, and acceptable according to this passage?

3. Why is it so difficult for us to believe that we measure up apart from our accomplishments?

4. When we base our sense of self on our performance, we tend to either be too hard on ourselves (insecure) or too prideful (arrogant). Do you tend to punish yourself when you don't perform well, or celebrate yourself too much when you do? Feel free to give a recent example.

5. In *The Wild Man* fable, the Wild Man enjoys his strength but doesn't need to prove to himself or other people that he measures up. How does this free him up to serve and protect other people?

Pray

Close in prayer asking God to open your eyes to the ways that you are trying to measure up through your performance and achievements. Ask your Father in Heaven to convince your heart that you fully measure up by grace, and not by the works you do.

Challenge for the Week

Pray each day this week for each member of your tribe that
God would help them live by grace instead of performance.

Week 4

Owning Up

Read Aloud

> Hardly anything else reveals so well the fear and uncertainty among men as the length to which they will go to hide their true selves from each other and even from their own eyes. – A.W. Tozer, *That Incredible Christian*[13]

> "There is nothing that binds us so firmly as the chains we have broken." – Howard Thurman

> "Whoever conceals his transgressions will not prosper, but he who confesses and forsakes them will obtain mercy." – Proverbs 28:13

Near my house in central Nebraska, the deer have created a network of game trails along the Platte River. Whitetails typically walk the same path as they move from their beds to their feeding ground, wearing a deep rut into the soft, sandy soil. Once a game trail is established, deer rarely take a different route. They are creatures of habit.

We also are creatures of habit, and many of us have chosen hurtful paths of thought and lifestyle that we have a hard time escaping. We all mess up. Many of us have made choices that we regret, but inexplicably, we continue to make them over and over again. We long to change, but our feet feel cemented by shame to the same futile paths.

It doesn't need to be this way. We can leave our old ways for a new trail. But there is only one way to do this—to jump the ruts and follow the path of life we must be honest about our sins.

To journey to the Wild Mountain, we need to own up to who we are and what we've done. No more blaming our past. No more blaming other people. No more blaming our habits, addictions, genetics, and history. To walk with God as fearless men begins with humility and confession. It begins with owning up. Only then will we be ready to forge new trails.

For Discussion

1. Have someone read 1 John 1:9.

The path to forgiveness and righteousness is simple, but many men struggle to take it. Why do you think it is so difficult for men to be honest with God and others about their sins and weaknesses?

2. How does owning up to our sins help us feel close to God again?

3. How does feeling close to God help us want to walk in the paths of righteousness, saying no to sin and temptation?

4. What are a few of the common ruts that men fall into today? How does *The Wild Man* fable illustrate a few of these cultural problems?

5. Do you believe you can leave your ruts once and for all by confessing your sins and walking in the grace of God? Why, or why not?

Pray

Have one of the older men in your tribe read Psalm 51:1-5.

Close in prayer together by reading aloud this Prayer of Confession by John Calvin:

"Lord God, eternal and Almighty Father: We acknowledge before your holy Majesty that we are poor sinners, conceived and born in guilt and in corruption, prone to do evil, unable of our own power to do good. Because of our sin, we endlessly violate your holy commandments. But, O Lord, with heartfelt sorrow we repent and turn away from all our offenses. We condemn ourselves and our evil ways, with true sorrow asking that your grace will relieve our distress. Have compassion on us, most gracious God, Father of mercies, for the sake of your son Jesus Christ our Lord. And in removing our guilt, also grant us daily increase of the grace of your Holy Spirit, and produce in us the fruits of holiness and of righteousness pleasing in your sight: Through Jesus Christ our Lord.

Amen."

Challenge for the Week

The challenge for this week is to ask for forgiveness from someone in your life you have wronged or hurt. As you go through the week, look for the opportunity to own up to your sin or offense by gently and humbly asking for forgiveness.

Week 5

Fleeing The Seductive Stranger

Read Aloud

"When we sinful men come together in Christ's presence for confession, he unites us as the brotherhood of his cross. Our most inexcusable sin, once nailed to his blood-soaked cross, loses its damning power forever." - Ray Ortlund, *The Death of Porn*[14]

"God does not 'hate' sex; he hates faithless sex with forbidden women, but he loves faithful sexual expressions in the context of marriage. God loves it so much that he commands, not just that it happen, but that it be enjoyed to the point of intoxication." – Heath Lambert, *Finally Free*[15]

"For the lips of a forbidden woman drip honey, and her speech is smoother than oil, but in the end she is bitter as wormwood, sharp as a two-edged sword." – Proverbs 5:3-4, ESV

If you feel dirty, you'll likely stay dirty. If you feel dirty, you'll likely choose to get dirtier. Why not? If you're already a mess, why not get messier?

This is what using pornography and entertaining lustful thoughts does to us. It makes us feel soiled, ashamed, and unlovable. It doesn't matter that the world tells us pornography is harmless. It doesn't matter how many times we hear the message, "Boys will be boys. It's OK." When we use porn, we feel dirty.

In *The Wild Man* fable, the Wild Man lives free in a way that many men long for but can barely imagine. He stands on the Looking Rock, breathing crisp, mountain air deep into his lungs. He roars. He feasts. He wrestles bears for pleasure. But, he also enjoys a clear conscience. **As men, the pleasure of feeling clean and whole and right with the Lord is a large part of enjoying our salvation and our masculinity.**

No matter what our experiences with pornography have been, the Gospel beckons us to believe that God can change us. We can be forgiven. We can be set free. Importantly, we can stay free. Not by installing filters on our computers or content-blockers on our phones (as helpful as those things are), but by understanding and believing the Gospel. We should fill our minds with the biblical story and learn the truths of who Christ is and what He has done for us. Jen Wilkin writes, "The heart cannot love what the mind does not know. Right thinking will beget right feeling."[16]

This must be our "strategy" for walking in freedom from thinking lustful thoughts and using pornography: we must learn of Christ through the Scriptures and believe in the love of God toward us. The more we enjoy God's grace and mercy, the more our hearts desire Him instead of sin.

My friend, you can ascend the Wild Mountain, climb the Looking Rock, and roar the roar of freedom. The power that raised Christ from the dead gives you victory over pornography and sexual temptation of every kind.

For Discussion

1. In the fable, the Seductive Stranger had a cluster of lifeless men in his, or her, shadow. How does our involvement with pornography and sexual immorality steal our joy and put us in the shadows?

2. Have someone read 2 Corinthians 7:8-11.

What role do godly sorrow and repentance play in helping us feel clean?

3. What are some ways that we can help one another as men turn from pornography and lust in all forms to pursue faithfulness to Jesus?

4. Have someone read Philippians 4:8.

Practically speaking, what does it look like to take our lustful thoughts captive, and redirect them toward the good, true, and beautiful?

5. Do you believe that it is possible, by God's grace and help, not to sin in these areas of sexual temptation?

6. Have someone read Romans 6:7, 14.

What do these two verses tell us about the possibility of never sinning again in these areas?

Pray

Pray together that God would convince you of the life-changing power of the Gospel, and show you how, by grace, you can live a life that is free from pornography.

Challenge for the Week

Read Proverbs 5 each day this week and ask God to give you the strength and wisdom to say no to sexual temptation.

Week 6

A Wild Man's View of Women

Read Aloud

"God assigns as a duty to every man the dignity of every woman." – Pope John Paul II

"God made humanity in his image as both male and female, which reflects the harmony and relationality of the Trinity, supplies the foundation for the different roles and responsibilities of men and women, was reaffirmed in the life of Jesus Christ, and cannot be reinvented or dissolved by new cultural standards." - Claire Smith, *Humanity as Male and Female*[17]

"So God created man in his own image, in the image of God he created him; male and female he created them." – Genesis 1:27, ESV

Throughout the centuries, in almost every civilization, women have been taken advantage of and exploited. Yet the boy or man seeking to be like Jesus will recognize the equal value and honor God has assigned to the women in his life.

Jesus' interactions with women throughout the Gospels is truly revolutionary. He affirmed their worth and dignity in how He spoke to them (Cf. John 8:10-11, Luke 7:12-13), cared for them (Cf. Luke 13:10-17), and illustrated his teachings with them as exemplars (Luke 15:8-10, Luke 21:1-4).

Jesus' treatment of women is theologically consistent with Genesis' account of Creation. God created both male and female in His image. He created them to be equals in value and worth. And He gave them both the Great Commandment to, "be fruitful and multiply and fill the earth and subdue it."[18]

An aspect of God's perfect design involved creating Adam and Eve in different ways, in part to display their complementary distinctions. In Genesis 2:20, when God called Eve Adam's "helper," He ascribed to all women an honorable title. The Hebrew word in Genesis 2:18 that we translate into "helper" is a title that God often uses to describe Himself. For example, in Psalm 33:20, the Psalmist says, "Our soul waits for the LORD; he is our *help* and our shield."

The word "help" in Psalm 33:20 is the same word God uses to describe Eve in Genesis 2:18. "Helper" is an honorable label, celebrating the indispensable importance of women in our lives as men.

What's more, through the process of creation described in Genesis 1-2, God shows us that women are to be cherished. Eve represents all humanity in the story of Creation. As Adam was delighted by Eve, God is displaying how He is delighted with humanity. As Eve was made from Adam, we as humanity were made from God (by God). As Eve was made of the same stuff - the human essence - we were created by God "in His image." Though not God, we are made by God to relate to Him and share certain attributes with Him.

The very story of Creation shows the equal value and importance of women and men, even as it shows our different roles and responsibilities.

As wild men, we must roar into the face of our culture, or into the face of savage men, who threaten to degrade or devalue the women in our lives. We must also speak up against those who seek to diminish the beautiful distinctions between men and women, male and female.

And if we are especially wise, we will seek out and gladly receive the help and counsel that the women and girls in our lives offer; it is a gift given to us directly from God.

For Discussion

1. What are a few ways that our society makes women feel vulnerable, taken advantage of, or devalued?

2. Have someone read 1 Peter 3:7.

"Weaker vessels" in this verse mostly refers to how men, in general, are physically stronger than women. Peter may also be pointing to the vulnerability that women often experience in society because of various structures and cultural norms.
    With that in mind, what does it look like for us men to treat women as equals, while owning our responsibility to care for, serve, and protect them?

3. In our first tribal meeting, we discussed the difference between being wild and being savage. How do you think that wild men will treat women differently than savage men?

4. How can we help the women in our lives - our daughters, sisters, wives and/or girlfriends, mothers – flourish?

5. Describe a friend or father figure who has shown you a truly masculine attitude toward women.

Pray

Pray together that God would help you view the women in your life as your Father in Heaven views them.

Challenge for the Week

The challenge for the week is for each man to pick one woman—young or old— and ask her this question:
Please describe a man who makes you feel valued and honored. How does he make you feel this way?

Week 7

Fleeing The Foolishly Fun Stranger

Read Aloud

"The satisfactions of manifesting oneself concretely
in the world through manual competence have been
known to make a man quiet and easy...
...Boasting is what a boy does, because he has no
real effect in the world." – Matthew B. Crawford, *Shop
Class as Soul Craft*[19]

"When I was a child, I spoke like a child, I thought
like a child, I reasoned like a child. When I became a
man, I gave up childish ways." – 1 Corinthians 13:11,
ESV

We are seeing an epidemic of irresponsible boys and men
today. Boys—often in their 20's, 30's, and 40's—drift from job
to job, watching television or playing video games all night,
while trying to meet their relational needs through social
media and their sexual needs through pornography. The
percentage of men in the workforce has dropped from 97% in
1967, to 88% in 2022.

What are men doing all day?

According to national surveys, they're spending most
of their time "socializing, relaxing, and at leisure."[20] Meaning,
more and more boys and men are shirking responsibility to
play with their toys, games, and hobbies.

To live as wild men, we must trade in our childish
habits for the mindset of masculinity. We must choose to be
responsible. To do our work. To honor our commitments. To

take care of what is necessary before we rest or play.

This mindset of masculinity takes a tremendous discipline of the will but leads to the pleasure of productivity. Harry Emerson Fosdick writes,

> "No horse gets anywhere until he is harnessed. No steam or gas ever drives anything until it is confined. No Niagara is ever turned into light and power until it is tunneled. No life ever grows great until it is focused, dedicated, disciplined."

God made us to contribute to our community. Our fundamental endeavor as people created in the image of God is to work, cultivate, and create in ways that bring honor to the One who made us. There is a time and a place for having fun, but if that's all we exist for, we're living foolish lives.

For Discussion

1. In *The Wild Man* fable, the Foolishly Fun Stranger also had a group of lifeless men in his shadow. How does being irresponsible steal our joy and put us in the shadows?

2. When do you feel most tempted to set aside your responsibilities to play and have fun?

3. Who does it most affect, or hurt, when you play too much or too often?

4. Who in your life is a good example of a man who knows how to work and contribute, yet have fun at appropriate times? Describe this man.

5. Have someone read 1 Corinthians 13:11-12.

In these two verses, Paul connects giving up childish ways

with seeing God one day face-to-face. How does the fact that we will be with the Lord soon cause us to stay focused, diligent, and responsible right now?

Pray

Pray together that God would give you the wisdom to know when it's time to work and serve others, and when it's appropriate to play and relax.

Close your time together by reading aloud this prayer by Thomas à Kempis:

> "Most gracious God, preserve us from the cares of this life, lest we should be too much entangled therein; also from the many necessities of the body, lest we should be ensnared by pleasure; and from whatever is an obstacle to the soul, lest, being broken with troubles, we should be overthrown. Give us strength to resist, patience to endure, and constancy to persevere; for the sake of Jesus Christ our Lord and Savior. Amen."

Challenge for the Week

The challenge for the week is to pick three chores, or home or auto repair issues, that you have been putting off… and do them. Report your results to your Tribe next week.

Week 8

Warriorhood

Read Aloud

"Strength is the ability to move or stand against external forces. Courage is kinetic. Courage initiates movement, action or fortitude. Courage exercises strength. The 'cowardly lion' - the tough looking guy who stands aside as weaker men fight the fight, take the risks and do the work - is worth less than the men who step into the arena." – Jack Donovan, *The Way of Men*[21]

"They shall be like mighty men in battle,
trampling the foe in the mud of the streets;
they shall fight because the Lord is with them,
and they shall put to shame the riders on horses."
- Zechariah 10:5, ESV

"Be watchful, stand firm in the faith, act like men, be strong." – 1 Corinthians 16:13, ESV

The Apostle Paul says in 1 Corinthians 16:13 that we are to, "act like men."

What does that mean? That's one of the great questions our culture is trying to answer today. Considering Paul as a man, clearly, this isn't a command to be savage or brutish. Paul would not tell us to talk tough, walk with our chests puffed out, or be controlling and demanding of others. Paul wasn't that kind of man, so he certainly isn't encouraging us to be either. No, when Paul tells us to, "act like men," he's telling us to be masculine as Jesus was masculine. Jesus is Paul's example for everything, including how to act like a man.

When we look to Jesus, we see a warrior who is both strong and tender. He's driven by His commitment to be faithful to His Father, and by His sincere love for other people. As a warrior, Jesus humbled Himself, leaving the infinite pleasures of heaven to come to earth on a rescue mission. As a warrior, He saw our need, and at great personal cost—His life—He provided a way for us to be made righteous and gain eternal life. As a warrior, He didn't fear men, or what they might do to Him. As a warrior, He stood for justice, rescuing the mistreated, elevating the marginalized, and caring for those in need. And as a warrior, He tenderly and courageously addressed untruths in His culture, because ideas that are false steal life and joy.

As we discussed last week, wild men do not live as if this world is a playground for their distraction and amusement. One of the reasons God has called us to work and serve is that there are so many people in this world who need us to be warriors, as Jesus was a warrior. Orphans in Haiti, Uganda, and China need us to be warriors. Young boys and girls in the sex-slave industry in Africa, the Middle East, Asia, and in our own country need us to be warriors. The Afghanistan and Ukrainian refugees showing up on our shores need us to be warriors. Single mothers, children in the foster care system, the sick, and the poor need us to be warriors as Jesus was a warrior.

For Discussion

1. Have someone read 1 Corinthians 16:13-14.

In these two verses, Paul connects acting like men with doing everything in love. How does being a warrior like Jesus enable us to love the people in our lives?

2. In *The Wild Man*, the men are hiding in the shadows of the cellar. When Balen wants to do the right thing, they encourage him to "do nothing." Do you recognize this attitude in our culture today? If so, how does it show up?

3. Can you think of a time that you stood up for, or cared for, a poor, mistreated, marginalized, or vulnerable person? Describe that moment and how you felt when you were faithful.

4. Jesus said, "And do not fear those who kill the body but cannot kill the soul. Rather fear him who can destroy both soul and body in hell. (Matt. 10:28)" How does fearing God help us not fear man?

5. In addition to Jesus, describe one person—perhaps a character from a book or a movie—who demonstrates warriorhood.

Pray

Pray together that God would give you the heart of a warrior.

Challenge for the Week

The challenge for the week is for your tribe to make a financial contribution to an organization that is caring for widows, orphans, foster children, or refugees (Cf. Compassion International – www.compassion.com, International Justice Mission – www.ijm.org, Samaritan's Purse – www.samaritanspurse.org, or Show Hope – www.showhope.org).

Along with donating, have each member of your tribe pray for that organization each day this week.

Week 9

The Great Will Kneel

Read Aloud

> "Do you wish to rise? Begin by descending. You plan a tower that will pierce the clouds? Lay first the foundation of humility." – Augustine

> "Not everyone can be famous but everyone can be great because greatness is determined by service. You only need a heart full of grace and a soul generated by love." – Martin Luther King, Jr.

> "But whoever would be great among you must be your servant, and whoever would be first among you must be slave of all." – Mark 10:43b-44, ESV

In *The Wild Man* fable, Balen doesn't go looking for greatness; he seeks only to protect his village. However, because he courageously put others first, he was given the awesome responsibility of becoming a Wild Man. This is precisely the path to becoming great in the kingdom of God—when our goal is to serve, not be served, we display the values and qualities of our Savior.

The world tells us that we demonstrate our worth by getting into the end zones of life, and then demanding that the camera be pointed at us while we perform our victory dances. According to the world, we prove our success and importance through scoring baskets, acing tests, earning large incomes, and owning expensive possessions.

God's definition of greatness is completely different. In

Matthew 20:26, Jesus said, "Whoever wants to be great among you must be your servant."

With this statement, Jesus didn't merely tweak the world's power structures; He dismantled them.

"Servant" isn't a glamorous title. Servants wash feet, scrub toilets, change diapers, do the dishes, help with homework, mow the lawn, clean up cat puke, and rub tired necks at the end of long days. Servants work behind the scenes, and when the cameras aren't rolling. Servants live to please their Master. And servants aim, not at displaying their greatness, but at showcasing the excellence of Jesus, as John the Baptist declared, "[The Christ] must increase, but I must decrease."[22]

This is how Jesus was great. And this is the path to greatness all wild men must follow.

For Discussion

1. Have someone read Luke 22:27.

What are some of the ways that Jesus served His friends and family?

2. What role did suffering play in Jesus' service to us?

3. What are ways we might suffer if we make ourselves servants of the people in our lives? Are you willing to suffer in these ways?

4. Do you struggle with the idea of being a servant? What is it about these ideas that pose a challenge?

5. Describe a man or woman in your life who follows Jesus' example of true greatness. What do you admire and respect about him/her?

Pray

Have someone in your tribe read Galatians 5:13.

Pray together that God will redefine greatness in your minds and hearts and give you opportunities to serve other people this week.

Challenge for the Week

The challenge for this week involves two tasks:

1. Give some amount of money to someone in need anonymously and/or do something kind for someone without drawing attention to yourself.

2. Pick one of the dirtiest, grossest, or most undesirable chores in your home or workplace, and do it with gladness knowing that you are following the example of Jesus, the greatest Wild Man to ever walk this earth.

Week 10

Willing to Stand Alone

Read Aloud

"Life always gets harder toward the summit – the cold increases, responsibility increases." – Friedrich Nietzsche, *Twilight of the Idols*

"Most of the world's great souls have been lonely. Loneliness seems to be one price the saint must pay for his saintliness." – A.W. Tozer, *Man-The Dwelling Place of God*[23]

"And he who sent me is with me. He has not left me alone, for I always do the things that are pleasing to him." – John 8:29, ESV

The Gospel story is filled with tales of lonely men, courageous leaders who, because they followed the call of God, were abandoned, maligned, misunderstood, and even killed. Noah. Moses. David. Many of the Prophets. John the Baptist. Jesus. The Apostle Paul. All these men walked with God in an ungodly world and paid a high relational price for it.

Loneliness can feel like severe pain. Over the ages, many prisoners have endured horrific forms of physical torture, only to finally break when isolated through solitary confinement. If we are willing to be honest, many of us would admit that we would prefer to break our backs working for the kingdom of God rather than feel lonely or excluded from other people. Isolation is a particularly painful ache.

To be wild, we must be willing to be lonely. There's no

111

other way to be masculine than to be courageously faithful to God. Jesus has shown us that being faithful to God in this world means you will walk alone at times. When Jesus did what His Father wanted, his family thought he was crazy, his friends deserted him, and his countrymen, the Israelites, wanted Him dead. Jesus' faithfulness often caused His isolation.

But, Jesus was willing to go there.

And we must be willing to go there, as well.

At times today, uncompromising faithfulness to God will lead us to high, cold, dangerous peaks. Alone, yet always with the Lord.

For Discussion

1. Why do faithful, courageous leaders often end up lonely?

2. Why do you think that loneliness is one of the hardest pains to endure?

3. Can you describe a time when you did the right thing, but ended up alone because of it?

4. Can you describe a time when you gave in and compromised doing the right thing in order not to feel lonely?

5. Have someone read Romans 8:31-38.

As Christians, the love and presence of God never leaves us. How can this truth keep us from feeling utterly alone in those moments when no person stands with us?

Pray

Close in prayer asking God to give you the courage to be faithful, even if it means walking alone as a leader.

Challenge for the Week

The challenge for this week is to spend one hour this week alone with God (praying, reading Scripture, and perhaps journaling). No cell phones. No television. No friends. No distractions. Just an hour alone with God.

Week 11

"I've Got Your Back!"

Read Aloud

"The only thing that makes battle psychologically tolerable is the brotherhood among soldiers. You need each other to get by." – Sebastian Junger

"And Elijah said to Elisha, 'Please stay here, for the LORD has sent me as far as Bethel.' But Elisha said, 'As the LORD lives, and as you yourself live, I will not leave you.' So they went down to Bethel." – 2 Kings 2:2, ESV

My son struck out three times during his first kid-pitch baseball game. I spent most of the game trying to think of what I would say to lift his spirits on the ride home. When we got into the truck, he exclaimed with excitement, "That was such a fun game, Dad!"

I was shocked. I almost drove the pickup into a light pole. I pulled over and turned around to look at him. "What made it a fun game, buddy?"

He replied, "Didn't you see it? Carl got two hits! One went over the centerfielder's head!"

Carl is Aidan's best friend, and because he did well, Aidan had a great night.

As men, we often struggle to make life-giving friendships because we feel driven to find our significance through our accomplishments. This achievement-oriented view of self makes us view our friends as measuring sticks, people to outperform to feel good about ourselves. This self-focus destroys our chance at true brotherhood. We can't love and support people that we feel we need to beat.

As we discussed last week, there will be times when we will walk alone. But not always. God has designed us for life-giving, soul-strengthening friendships, and the only way we can find these relationships is if we're living by faith in the grace of God. When we realize that we are fully significant and acceptable because of the finished work of Christ, we can quit looking at our performance and achievements to feel like we measure up. This faith, this grace of God, enables us to truly celebrate our friends' successes and mourn their losses.

For Discussion

1. What are some ways that you have tried to best your friends to feel good about yourself? (I.e. through sports, work, academics, or possessions?)

2. Have someone read 1 Corinthians 13:1-7.

How does the grace of God enable us to love others and enjoy solid, supportive friendships?

3. Have someone read Proverbs 17:17.

Describe a time when a friend helped you go through a hard or stressful situation.

4. In *The Wild Man* fable, the Wild Man and the Ancient Man have a profound friendship. What role did their mission and work play their forming such significant bonds?

5. What are some things you most appreciate about your friendships?

6. What are some things you'd like to see changed about your

friendships?

Pray

Have someone in your tribe read 1 Samuel 18:1-5.

Pray together that God would give you an awareness of grace so sincere that it enables you to truly love and support your friends.

Challenge for the Week

The challenge for this week is to write one friend a letter telling him what you most appreciate about him.

Week 12

Choosing Heroes Carefully

Read Aloud

"Our culture has filled our heads but emptied our hearts, stuffed our wallets but starved our wonder. It has fed our thirst for facts but not for meaning or mystery. It produces 'nice' people, not heroes."
– Peter Kreeft, *Jesus-Shock*[24]

"Brothers, join in imitating me, and keep your eyes on those who walk according to the example you have in us." – Philippians 3:17, ESV

"Do not be deceived: 'Bad company ruins good morals.'" – 1 Corinthians 15:33, ESV

The term "hero" comes from the ancient Greeks. A hero was someone who did something greater than what "normal humanity" was doing. Hercules performed twelve nearly impossible Labors. Achilles was the finest warrior of the Trojan War. Theseus was the Athenian hero who liberated his city from the tyranny of King Minos of Crete and his monstrous Minotaur. All three men were considered heroes because they stretched people's sense of possibility. They did more than those around them and made others believe, "If my hero can do great things, perhaps I can as well."

We need heroes today. We need examples of men who embody the qualities and virtues we would like to possess. As men aspiring to be wild and masculine, we need to find people who represent various aspects of Christ—courage, justice, sacrifice, love, and honor—and we need to watch them, be inspired by them, and imitate them.

The question isn't whether we will choose heroes. The question is whether we will choose the right ones. If heroes give us vision and then challenge us to imitate them, then we need to select the type of men we want to become. If we make a crass, vulgar man our hero, we will move toward crassness and vulgarity. Immanuel Kant said, "From the crooked timber of humanity, no straight thing was ever made."

As Wild Men, we should choose men who are kind, hard-working, and honest to imitate. We should be drawn to men who are faithful to God and devoted to loving other people. If we follow and imitate truly masculine men, by God's grace and help, we will become masculine ourselves.

For Discussion

1. Who are some of your heroes? Explain why.

2. Can you describe some of the ways that you have become like the men you most admire?

3. Have someone read Hebrews 11:13-16.

Hebrews 11 is often referred to as the "Heroes of the Faith" chapter. According to these verses, what makes a person a hero of the faith?

4. Apart from Jesus, our heroes will occasionally fail us. How can we use those moments of disillusionment to grow closer to God and deepen our faith?

5. Men at any age can be a hero to younger men. What are some ways in which the younger men in your tribe can be good and godly examples for the younger men in their lives?

Pray

Pray for one another that you would choose the right heroes and become the right kind of hero for other people.

Challenge for the Week

The challenge for this week is to pick one of your heroes and pray for him each day that God would help him continue to be faithful and masculine.

Week 13

Wild Means Obedient

Read Aloud

"We must all suffer one of two things: the pain of discipline or the pain of regret, or disappointment." – Jim Rohn

"Whatever your heart clings to and confides in, that is really your god." - Martin Luther, *You Are What You Love*[25]

"Blessed is everyone who fears the LORD, who walks in his ways! You shall eat the fruit of the labor of your hands; you shall be blessed, and it shall be well with you." – Psalm 128:1-2, ESV

It's time to live a wild, truly masculine life. The path forward for us is clear: we must fear the Lord, love His Word, and choose His ways over the ways of this world. To be wild, we must walk in the wisdom of God's designs, not fight against them. H.H. Farmer said, "If you go against the grain of the universe, you get splinters."

Most of us are going through *The Wild Man* 14-week journey because we want to live free, strong, masculine lives. Most of us would say that we love God above all things.

But... not everyone who goes through this journey will enjoy a truly *wild* existence. It's not because we don't understand these ideas; it's because we aren't willing to bend our knees and submit ourselves to the authority of God our Father. It's because we're not choosing to love and obey God

123

rather than loving and obeying our wants and desires.

The great mystery that some of us will discover, but many will miss, is that true freedom and joy in life is found in submitting our heart, mind, soul, and strength to God as our King. We must deny self and continually choose to obey God no matter whether we fully understand, or initially enjoy, His commands. We must believe that He is Lord, and He is perfect in His plans for us. He leads. We follow, trusting that He alone knows the path to human flourishing.

Perhaps it helps to consider the words of the great football coach, Tom Landry: "The job of a football coach is to make men do what they do not want to do in order to achieve what they always wanted to be."

All that we hope to be as men - Wild men - is only possible when we, as James K.A. Smith writes, "(regularly) calibrate our hearts, tuning them to be directed to the Creator, our magnetic north."[26]

For Discussion

1. Have someone read Romans 6:17-23.

According to the Apostle Paul, is it possible not to be a slave to something? Can anyone actually be "their own man" in a way that they don't serve some master?

2. What does it look like for us to be "slaves of God" (Romans 6:22)?

3. Can you describe a man who lives a strong, humble life under the authority of God?

4. Describe an area of your life that you are trying to "go against the grain of the universe," by doing things your way instead of God's way.

5. What would it look like to submit to the Lord in that area, and choose to live according to His ways?

6. Elton Trueblood said, "Discipline is the price of freedom."

For the older men in the tribe: How has this proven true throughout your lifetime?

Pray

Pray together that God will give you a vision of what it looks like to submit to His authority and choose to obey His commands.

Challenge for the Week

The challenge for this week is to start each day this week on your knees with your face on the floor, praying that God will give you a heart to submit to Him.

Week 14

Torch-Bearing

Read Aloud

> "A man who 'cannot get it together' is a man who has probably not had the opportunity to undergo ritual initiation into the deep structures of manhood. He remains a boy - not because he wants to, but because no one has shown him the way to transform his boy energies into man energies." - Robert Moore & Douglas Gillette, *The Crisis in the Masculine Ritual Process*[27]

> "I believe that what we become depends on what our fathers teach us at odd moments, when they aren't trying to teach us. We are formed by little scraps of wisdom." – Umberto Eco

> "…and what you have heard from me in the presence of many witnesses entrust to faithful men who will be able to teach others also." – 2 Timothy 2:2, ESV

Remember the days when men were men? They dressed in self-respect and style. They honored their elders. They opened doors for women and greeted each other with strong handshakes. They worked hard and took pride in their careers. And they weren't afraid to move out of their parent's house, get married, remain faithful to their wife, have children, and teach their children how to grow up big and strong. Remember those days? You might not… they were quite some time ago.

Today, more and more boys are refusing to travel the ancient paths of masculinity, in large part because more and more men are failing to show them the way.

In *The Wild Man* fable, the Ancient Man enjoyed the thrill of initiating Balen (Aidan). A wild man doesn't merely enjoy his masculinity; he also empowers younger men to enjoy theirs as well. All truly wild men take their responsibility to instruct, correct, rebuke, and train others as seriously as they take their call to be wild. Indeed, the two tasks are the same.

We older men must teach the young men in our lives how to join us. We must be wild and give them a vision of true masculinity. Stephen Mansfield writes, "All it takes for a contagious manly culture to form is for one genuine man to live out a genuine manhood."[28]

We must be the torchbearers a new generation of wild men need us to be.

For Discussion

1. Describe one or two men who have been torchbearers for you, helping cast a vision for wild masculinity.

2. Describe a few opportunities that you currently have to be a torchbearer to other men.

3. Many older men do not feel adequate to be torchbearers for younger men. What are some reasons why older men are disengaging from this responsibility?

4. Older men can only teach and cast a vision for masculinity if they are willing to spend time with younger men. What are some obstacles that seem to prevent older men and younger men from spending time together?

5. Have someone read Deuteronomy 6:4-9.

What role does God's Word play in how we older men pass along masculinity to younger men?

Pray

Pray for the desire and the opportunity to be faithful torchbearers.

Challenge for the Week

The challenge for this week...

1. ...for the younger men: Write your future self a letter describing a few of the lessons God has taught you over the past fourteen weeks about being a faithful, wild man. (Consider writing the letter on the "Notes" pages at the end of this book.)
      In the letter, describe what you appreciated about the Wild Man or Ancient Man who brought you to the Tribe each week. Read this letter on your 25th birthday.

2. ...for the older men: Pick up an extra copy of *The Wild Man* to give as a gift to a friend. Before you give it to him, write a note on the inside of the book challenging him to be a Torch-Bearing Wild Man.

Wild Mountain Feast

Unlike other adventures, our journey to the Wild Mountain never ends. We like checklists. We like to make a box, mark a check through it, and declare, "I'm done. Time to move on to the next box."

We must resist the urge to think this way about our journey toward masculinity. The second we stop growing and changing is the moment we cease to be wild. A truly masculine man seeks to be more faithful and masculine tomorrow than he is today.

That being said, we have traveled far together through difficult terrain. We have ascended the Wild Mountain and it's time to celebrate. It's time to slow down and enjoy the view together. It's time to feast together. **Most importantly, it's time for us older men to initiate the young men in our tribe into the fraternity of wild men.**

There is great freedom within each tribe to personalize this Wild Mountain Feast. Depending on your interests, you may make or buy personal gifts, add various rituals, and plan a meal that you most enjoy. For some, the Wild Mountain Feast might consist entirely of meat. For others, it might involve seven courses. Plan the meal in the way your tribe prefers.

For your consideration, here are a few suggestions for your Wild Mountain Feast:

Have the Older Serve the Younger: The older men should plan the evening, choose the location and menu, and serve the younger men. You might hold the feast in a restaurant, at a state park, or in a backyard.

Give a Gift: The initiation from boyhood into manhood is a life-changing event, one that the young men will remember the rest of their lives. Consider giving each young man a gift that will last the rest of their lives.

This could be a homemade knife if you're a metal worker, a cutting board if you're a woodworker or chef, a shotgun if you're a hunter, or a hammer if you're a carpenter. The goal isn't to give an expensive gift, necessarily; it's to pass along something personal and meaningful.

Acknowledge a Quality: Have each older man in your tribe write a short letter to each younger man acknowledging one trait that they most respect about him. Give these letters as a gift during the celebration.

Pronounce a Blessing: At one point in *The Wild Man* fable, the Ancient Man "expressed his respect for Balen. He hugged him and blessed him against all upcoming trials."

Have each older man read a passage of Scripture and pray a blessing upon the young man he journeyed with to the Wild Mountain. Pray for him against all the struggles, trials, failures, and successes he has ahead of him.

This Scripture and blessing could be written down and given to the young man during the celebration.

Acknowledgments

I am immeasurably thankful to my two beautiful, bright-eyed daughters, Kate and Claire. These young women stake claim to just as much territory in my heart as does their brother Aidan. Yet, to complete this project I had to spend a disproportionate amount of time thinking specifically about how to parent Aidan. Kate and Claire never complained about this imbalance. They consistently displayed excitement and support for this project. I'm also amazed at their ability to keep a secret—they knew about this writing project for two years and managed to keep Aidan in the dark until I gave him these books on his twelfth birthday.

I'm grateful for Ellie. I started praying for Aidan's bride-to-be before I wrote the first version of this book in 2010. Ellie is the better-than-imagined answer God has given to these prayers.

This book for men would be missing many of its insights had it not been for the wise contributions of my wife, Jamie. My favorite time of the day these past two years has been when Jamie and I make dinner together and sort through the things of life. Many of the ideas in *The Wild Man* were fleshed out with her over a cutting board, the smell of garlic, and while Van Morrison, Bon Iver, or Andrew Peterson played in the background. Jamie is my true companion, and to quote Van, "the heavens open every time she smiles."[29]

I want to acknowledge my mother for her support and contribution. While my mom and I, in many ways, share the same soul, we hold vastly different worldviews. I am a Christian and a conservative who primarily writes about theology and men's issues. She is a Buddhist and a progressive who has been a strong voice within the feminist movement. Her writing, such as the New York Times bestseller, *Reviving Ophelia*, focuses on psychology and women's issues. Yet my mom has read, edited, and zealously supported each one of my writing projects, including *The Wild Man*.

I thank the Lord for *my* TRIBE of men and boys: Matt Green and his sons Kalob, Elijah, and Micah - Steve Strobel and his son Christian - Jason Swantek and his sons Garrett and Stone - Paul Huenefeld and his grandson Gabe. These brothers in Christ went through *The Wild Man* with me and my son Aidan. We met at Strobel's cabin, where we were often interrupted by geese landing on the lake or white bass hammering shad just off the beach. My heart is permanently bonded to the Wild Men of the **Bellator Tribe**.

There are several Wild Men and Ancient Men who have put flesh on the abstract idea of masculinity for me: Bryan Clark, Tom Osborne, Orv Qualsett, Scott Johnson, Mark Chidister, Larry Austin, and my father-in-law, RB Drickey.

A few of these men are bald, yet all of them are Wild. They are some of the best men I've ever known.

I want to express my love and gratitude for Jim Pipher, my dad. He gave me his love for music, Royals baseball, and Kansas City barbecue. He taught me how to pitch a baseball, tell a joke, and oppose racist and sexist comments. When my dad and I hug these days, it's cheek to cheek and beard to beard. In these recent years, especially, he's been an inexhaustible well of support for me, my wife Jamie, and our three kids. In his song, *Astral Weeks*, Van Morrison sings about a place, "where immobile steel rims crack."[30]

I have glimpsed this place – it's my dad's heart. The years have more than cracked the steel, they've turned it into something warm and safe.

I am grateful to Heartland's elders, pastors, and staff.

These friends gave me the time and encouragement to write *The Wild Man*.

I'm thankful for my readers: JJ Springer, Bryan Clark, Nathan Musgrave, Travis Purkerson, Robert Seeger, and Matt Mitchell. These friends helped turned lead into gold.

Or at least bronze.

Endnotes

1. Robert Bly. *Iron John: A Book About Men*, (Cambridge: Da Capo Press, 2004), 16

2. Sam Keen. *Fire in the Belly: On Being a Man*, (New York: Bantam Books, 1992), 28.

3. 1 John 2:14b-15, ESV

4. CS Lewis. *The Four Loves*, (New York: Harcourt Brace & Company, 1988), 66-67.

5. Proverbs 29:18, NASB

6. G.K. Chesterton. "The Red Angel," essay XVII in *Tremendous Trifles* (Public domain, 1909)

7. Robert Bly, "Thoughts" in *Morning Poems*, (New York: HarperCollins Publishers, 1997), 86

8. Andy Crouch. *Playing God: Redeeming the Gift of Power*, (Downers Grove: InterVarsity Press, 2013), 42

9. Dane Ortlund, *Want to Be Like Jesus? Be Gentle*, The Gospel Coalition website, October 17, 2018: www.thegospelcoalition.org/article/want-jesus-gentle/. Accessed February 2, 2024.

10. Robert Bly. *Iron John: A Book About Men*, (Cambridge: Da Capo Press, 2004), 93

11. Bryan Clark. *God's Not Like That*, (Colorado Springs: David C. Cook, 2023), 154-155

12. Ibid, 188.

13. A.W. Tozer. *That Incredible Christian*, (Wingspread Publishers, 1986)

14. Ray Ortlund. *The Death of Porn: Men of Integrity Building a World of Nobility*, (Wheaton: Crossway, 2021), 91.

15. Heath Lambert. *Finally Free: Fighting for Purity with the Power of Grace*, (Grand Rapids: Zondervan, 2013), 99.

16. Jen Wilkin. *Women of the Word: How to Study the Bible with Both our Hearts and Minds*, (Wheaton: Crossway, 2014), 33.

17. Claire Smith, *Humanity as Male and Female: An Essay*, The Gospel Coalition website: https://www.thegospelcoalition.org/essay/humanity-male-female/. Accessed February 16, 2024.

18. Genesis 1:28, ESV

19. Matthew B. Crawford. *Shop Class as Soul Craft: An Inquiry into the Value of*

Endnotes Cont.

Work, (New York: Penguin Group, 2009), 15

20. Micholas Eberstadt. *Men Without Work*, article taken from AEI (The American Enterprise Institute) website: https://www.aei.org/articles/men-without-work-2/. Accessed January 17, 2024.

21. Jack Donovan. *The Way of Men*, (Milwaukee: Jack Donovan, 2012), 31.

22. John 3:30, ESV.

23. A.W. Tozer. *The Saints Must Walk Alone*, chapter in "Man – The Dwelling Place of God," (Camp Hills: WingSpread, 1997)

24. Peter Kreeft. *Jesus-Shock*, (South Bend: Saint Augustine's Press, 2008)

25. Martin Luther. *Luther's Large Catechism*, translated by John Nicholas Lenker, (Minneapolis: Luther, 1908), 44.

26. James K.A. Smith. *You Are What You Love: The Spiritual Power of Habit*, (Grand Rapids: Brazos Press, 2016), 20.

27. Robert Moore and Douglas Gillette, *The Crisis in the Masculine Ritual Process*, ed. Keith Thompson, "To Be a Man: In Search of the Deep Masculine," Op. Cit., 43.

28. Stephen Mansfield. *Mansfield's Book of Manly Men*, (Nashville: Thomas Nelsen, 2013)

29. Van Morrison. *Crazy Love*, (Warner Bros. Records, 1970)

30. Van Morrison. *Astral Weeks*, (Warner Bros. Records, 1968)

Notes & Reflections

Notes & Reflections

Notes & Reflections

Notes & Reflections

Notes & Reflections

Notes & Reflections

Notes & Reflections

Notes & Reflections